PATCHWORK QUILTS

Averil Colby

B T BATSFORD LTD
LONDON

The front cover shows a nineteenth-century silk coverlet
made by Ann Hutton-Wilson, Yorkshire

© Averil Colby 1965

First Published 1965
Reprinted 1975
This paperback edition published 1988

ISBN 0 7134 5420 2

N. 137791

Printed and bound in Hong Kong
for the publishers B. T. BATSFORD LTD,
4 Fitzhardinge Street, London W1H 0AH

PATCHWORK QUILTS

Contents

Acknowledgment

The Author and Publishers would like to thank the following for kindly giving permission for examples of patchwork in their possession to be photographed and included in this book.

The American Museum in Britain, Bath. Pages 61, 67, 69, 75, 77
The Bowes Museum, Barnard Castle. Page 58
Mrs. Montague Carlisle. Page 87
Mrs. Marion Clifford. Page 89
Miss Dorothy Crampton. Pages 93, 95
Mr. John Franklin. Pages 47, 48
Miss Constance Hutton-Wilson. Page 54
Mrs. Ethel M. Wilson and Miss Dora Trowbridge. Page 44
The Trustees of the Victoria and Albert Museum. Pages 41, 43, 51

The Author and Publishers would like to thank the following for permission to reproduce photographs included in this book.

Mrs. Robin Bagot and the Trustees of the Victoria and Albert Museum. Page 33
Mrs. Mavis Fitz Randolph and The Rural Industries Bureau. Page 57
Mrs. Adèle Montague. Page 35
The National Museum of Wales. St. Fagan's Folk Museum. Page 71
The Royal Ontario Museum, Toronto, Canada. Page 83
The Shelburne Museum Inc., Shelburne, Vermont, United States of America. Pages 37, 39, 63, 73, 79
The Smithsonian Institution, Washington D.C. Page 53

Quilts illustrated on pages 64, 81, 85, 91 are from the Author's collection.

The Author would also like to thank Mrs. Norah Lee and Miss Dorothy Crampton for help with the drawings.

Introduction

A characteristic of English traditional patch-work during its best period from about 1780 until 1830—discounting the excellence of pattern and colour—was the economy in materials, time and work given to it. It is difficult to see why the methods used then to achieve such good results should have died out in favour of the less attractive work of the subsequent 100 years or so, which involved lengthy and tedious periods of cutting out and sewing several thousands of pieces for one bedspread, whether necessary or not. The number of pieces in one bedspread is quoted to this day as a matter of pride and some virtue, regardless of the fact that there may have been much needless waste of material in the process.

Too often also, insufficient planning and forethought have been given to making the best use of the materials available; if a little time could be given to this, before work on a bedspread is put in hand, much disappointment and much misdirected energy could be avoided. Patchwork is a traditional kind of needlework, primarily intended as an economy and so it should be looked upon still, but the fact that it has a tradition, gives a solid foundation on which each new work can be based and adapted to present-day materi-

als and ideas. This short study of traditional English patchwork, with some examples of American quilts and patterns, may not be amiss for a start—not to a kind of 'instant patchwork', but to reminders of some traditional short-cuts in avoiding unnecessary hard labour and waste of time and materials, which have been forgotten over the years.

The varying fortunes of the patchwork quilt in the needlework of the last three centuries have been influenced more directly than those of other kinds of embroidery by the changes of taste in fashion. If cotton were fashionable, then cotton went into the patch-work, if dark and sombre colours were being worn, they altered the appearance of quilts made for some years afterwards; the silks and velvet of the mid-nineteenth century pro-duced a kaleidoscope of rich colour but spelled ruin for most of the patchwork, and the later fashion for lilac, pink and pale blue sprigged cotton prints was responsible for so many quilts and bedspreads of patchwork, and their lasting quality was such that some are still intact and usable.

In all periods, traditional shapes and patterns have been used, but it was the kind and colour of the materials and—in the case of printed fabrics—the designs they con-

tained, that were all-important to the design of each quilt. Furnishing as well as dress-making pieces are traditional materials for patchwork, but of the two, dressmaking undoubtedly has contributed more to it since the early 1700s. This is especially so in patterns made entirely of geometrical shapes; and because so many examples of manu-factured textiles have been preserved in patchwork, when other traces of them have been lost sight of, quilts and coverlets have become of some value to the research and records of printed textiles, and of cotton in particular. By the evidence of surviving patchwork in England, it is known that work done in the early years of the eighteenth cen-tury, and in all probability some in the late 1600s also, contained remnants and cuttings of materials which not only were costly but hard to come by, and so every fragment was of value.

At the time when the import into England of the Indian painted calicoes was forbidden by Act of Parliament (passed on 29 September 1701), they were the most highly prized of all materials for dress and furnishing—to no small degree because they were forbidden —and the smallest scraps left over were pre-served for patchwork. Even so, a very large quantity would have been needed, as beds at that time were very wide, and in order to make the most of the coloured pieces a pro-portion of the work was made from the cheaper and more plentiful white or un-bleached calicoes. This imposed economic discipline and called for imagination and good planning, as well as an appreciation of space as a part of design, which can be seen in nearly all of the work made during the eighteenth century and the first 30 years of the nineteenth.

The earliest known example of English patchwork was made at Levens Hall near Kendal, in the County of Westmorland and it consists of a very large quilt and hangings made about 1708 from pieces of imported Indian prints, the whole work having survived in a remarkable state of preservation in the house in which it was made (p. 33). The work is composed of patches of five different shapes joined in a repetitive pattern, and so that nothing should be wasted, a num-ber of the shaped pieces was built up from several smaller fragments sewn together. The bedspread was quilted with red thread in an all-over diamond pattern, but the hangings are lined only; the whole set of hangings represents a unique record of dress and furnishing cottons of the household, which were fashionable from the end of the seventeenth century.

The introduction of the imported cotton prints changed the fashion in textiles, and later their influence revolutionised the print-ing of manufactured cottons and linens, as can be seen by the designs which were to be popular well into the nineteenth century. Perhaps the most notable among the Indian designs were the *palampores*, on which fruit-and flower-bearing trees, carrying birds and small animals among the branches, covered the whole of a bedspread or hanging; they were especially beautiful and a matching set of these furnishings for a bed was a coveted and rare possession, so the next best thing was one made of patchwork, as is evident by the Levens Hall work. That this was not just a passing fancy but something which became a fashion and lasted for at least a hundred years, can be seen by a set, com-plete with double valance on the tester, made between 1801 and 1804 and now in the

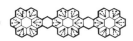

Castle Museum, Norwich, in Norfolk; but the cotton prints in this work were made from eighteenth-century and contemporary wood-block patterns. An American spread, known to have been made in the eighteenth century, also contains pieces of cottons 'probably cut...from one of the early... cottons imported from India'. This probability is borne out by the pattern, which not only bears some resemblance to the *tree* designs on the *palampores* but the birds and fruit may well have been cut from one of them (p. 39).

After the middle of the eighteenth century, surviving English and American patchwork shows many similar features in patterns, materials and methods of working. The very early pioneering days of the settlers in the New World were over, after more than a century of trade and traffic between the two countries, and printed cottons of English origin, fashionable and worn during the last 50 years of the century, can be seen in quilts and coverlets made during the period, in both England and America. Until 1752 all English textile colour printing had been done by hand by means of wood-blocks with some additional colouring put in by pencilling, but in Ireland, in this year, the process of printing from engraved copper plates was invented. Soon afterwards, the English factories were producing plate-printed cottons and linens, and by the last quarter of the century examples of monochrome plate prints found their way into patchwork; from time to time examples of them can be traced, although they do not appear to have been popular. This may have been due to the size and character of the designs, which generally were of large proportion and pictorial, with landscapes, figures and rustic scenes predom-

inating; also they lacked the variety of colour in which the block prints excelled. Some plate-printed cottons are included in the American *Star of Bethlehem* quilt, made towards the end of the eighteenth century (p. 37), and occasionally other examples are found, but although their influence on patchwork is slight, at least their presence in work of which the date is in question, establishes the fact that it was made later than 1752. A number of pictorial plate prints, commemorating scenes in American history, were printed in England for the American market from about 1800 and quilts containing examples of these naturally would be of a later nineteenth-century date.

There is no doubt, though, that the block-printed patterns set the fashion. The brilliance of the colours, the variety and quality in design, and the good wearing textures presented all the essentials needed for good patchwork and enabled it to hold its own with the most sophisticated embroidery. For the first time, perhaps, work with economy as its origin was a fashionable occupation and although 'poor man's embroidery' has been a label attached to patchwork, there was little that was poor in the work of the late eighteenth and early nineteenth centuries—in fact the tradition acquired new values then, which were to set a standard for all later work until the present day. The work was done by women in all walks of life regardless of social standing; the idea that it was 'cottage work' is true only in that cottage dwellers were as adept at making the patterns as the ladies in the manor and there is no doubt that the village dressmaker obtained many of her materials from working at the 'big house', so that the same piece bag supplied both cottage and manor. Ideas for pattern, also, shuttled

through a community in the same way, each worker putting on her own interpretation as she copied them, but from the evidence of examples of which we have the history, the work originated in the well-to-do households. It seems certain also, that it was common for the work on large furnishings to be shared by several members of the household; and although there appear to be no early written records, it is a matter of observation only to know that the many inequalities in eighteenth-century quilts and coverlets were due to the assistance of many hands in lightening the work. It is known to have been done in the nineteenth century and one of the earliest examples is that of a coverlet made by Jane and Cassandra Austen and their mother in 1811.

If other existing nineteenth-century records reflect what may be described as a traditional sideline in the history of patchwork, men as well as women and children probably had a hand in the work also—if not always with the sewing, at least with the planning. The precision of geometrical patterns appears to have drawn the interest of men towards patchwork, and time and again records and surviving work show that quilts and coverlets, and other work, have been designed and made by them. Generally their work is recognisable; the quilt designs follow the conventional arrangements but the distinguishing characteristic is that of many detailed and complex patterns in mosaic, following closely after one another, with the minimum of spacing between. Patterns in applied work seem to have had a limited attraction only and examples are scarce, but where they do occur the work usually is made of cloth, much of it said to have been of 'soldier's uniforms'. Of two

examples illustrated in which the work was planned by men, with nearly 100 years separating their making, it is difficult to say where the greatest credit should go—to the planners, or to their wives who were the makers, for their achievement in interpreting the intricacies of the designs in dress materials of their respective times—cottons between 1760 and 1785 (p. 35) and silks from about 1838 to 1842 (p. 54).

Whatever material was used, it seems that most workers appreciated the contrast of a light background for the strong, bright colours of the printed cottons, the proportion of each probably being governed by the supply of pieces to hand; but in all the patterns it is clear that care and economy were used, and much forethought put into the planning, so that unnecessary work in cutting out was avoided, and making sure at the same time that the materials were shown to their best advantage. This is especially clear in designs which include the use of applied as well as geometrical patterns.

Applied work is one of the oldest known means in needlework of decorating a plain surface and the virtue of its economy in doing so is of particular value in patchwork. The work involved, in proportion to the area covered by an applied pattern, is comparatively small, and the advantage of a ready-made design cut out from a coloured print is clear, especially to those who are more enthusiastic than industrious in achieving a result. But more than these considerations should be taken into account, as can be seen from the eighteenth-century examples in which respect for the materials and their designs, the careful cutting and arranging of them to make fresh patterns and the choice of method in which to apply them, reflect the appreciation of one

artist for the work of another. Flowered chintzes were used for dress as well as furnishings and these, together with the small-patterned cottons intended only for dressmaking, were used to make the geometrically shaped patches from the small cuttings left over from shaping the fashionably complicated sleeves and bodices. In many cases, this would have meant little more than trimming to make the required shapes, nearly all of which were based on a square. Squares themselves in all sizes were popular and so also were triangular shapes which could be cut from diagonally folded squares (1, 2). As a rule, designs on

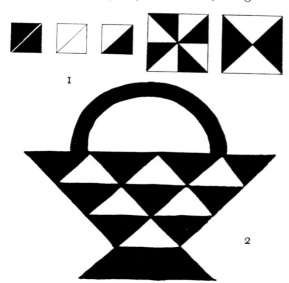

I

2

furnishing prints were of larger proportions and remnants from them probably would have been larger also, and the problem of cutting out and transferring them to a new background would have been comparatively simple; in the case of used materials which had become worn, it was an excellent method of preserving them.

3

Nearly all the quilts made during the last 20 years of the eighteenth century, and until about 1830, contained at least some applied patterns and in most of them the absorbing fascination of the flowered prints can be seen in the many ways in which they were introduced into the designs—with or without the addition of geometrical patterns. The printed patterns were treated in several

4

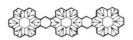

ways; often they were cut out as a whole motif, especially when the originals were sprays or bouquets of flowers (3, 4); *basket* patterns made from geometrical patchwork were filled with flowers cut out in the same way (5, 6) and baskets and cornucopias were cut from printed patterns and filled with flowers and fruit and occasionally a perching bird. Ingenious basket patterns were cut, probably with the help of a template, from prints with a design of trellis or lines on them, which gave the appearance of a basket weave and these, too, would contain floral motifs; in one instance a branching rose pattern in a basket supported an exotic type of pheasant on the topmost rose. In this pattern, as in many others, motifs and pieces were cut from a number of designs and reassembled to suit the worker's fancy, which had been taken often by the earlier Indian designs, but there seems to have been no end to the variety of ways in which floral cottons were introduced by hook or crook into the patchwork— as elaborate centre pieces, in bouquets filling in a corner, attached to curving stems with *leaves* and *buds* on narrow borders or decorating a whole bedspread, arranged as panels

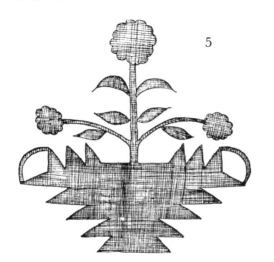

5

6

7

and borders with intervening spaces filled with small sprigs and florets (pp. 47, 48, 51).

Tree patterns composed of motifs cut from several prints are found occasionally and seem sometimes to be the excuse for inserting birds into the pattern. Bird patterns have been steadily popular in all periods, most of them having been cut directly from prints, but there are many examples of *birds* having been made up with skill and ingenuity from suitable coloured scraps of cotton intended to simulate body, wings and tail and so on (7, 8). The Lapwing or Green Plover is taken from a panel of a present-day work, completed in 1960 (p. 93). It has been common for flowers to be made up in this way, but arrangements of geometrical shapes, such as the *hexagon* or the *diamond*, were used as well as others of more realistic outline. Elliptical

a chintz pattern. Geometric flower patterns were more formal but recognisable floral motifs were made from them, sometimes with the assistance of a template-cut leaf or two added to the stem.

9

10

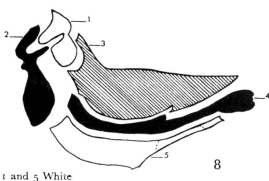

8

1 and 5 White
2 and 4 Black
3 Metallic green

shapes were popular for leaf shapes or flower petals (9, 10); imaginary flowers were cut in outline from template shapes (11) and often these were added to sprays of flowers cut from

11

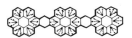

Many of the printed cottons contained patterns of ribbon; often it was tied in bows on bouquets of flowers, holding swags of fruit and flowers or other motifs and so ribbon too was introduced into patterns of applied work. Often strips of material were attached to the foundation in bow shapes and made to appear that they were tying the stems of flowers (3, 4), or else twisted into a chain as a frame for a centre pattern (p. 51.), or at other times a pattern in the shape of a bow was cut from a piece of print or plain coloured cotton and used as a motif on its own. Border patterns were made to represent swags and bows of ribbon cut from chintz and applied to a foundation, to which cords and tassels were added with embroidery (12). Geometric patches of rhomboid or rectangular shapes were used in alternating light and dark colours to give an illusion of folding ribbon as a border pattern (pp. 23, 24).

Great ingenuity as well as artistry went into making the applied patterns, which have added no little elegance to patchwork throughout its history, and the patterns were well matched by the methods used to sew them to their foundations. Many workers preferred to hem neatly round the turned-in edges of the motifs—a method which has been

13

used until to-day for all geometric or template shaped pieces. Designs cut from floral and other printed materials usually had an allowance of about $\frac{1}{4}$ inch left all round; this was turned in without paying too much attention to the detailed outline and hemmed down (13). Eighteenth- and nineteenth-century chintz patterns used for this method had been printed on a white or natural coloured ground, so that only the slightest definition marked the outline where one met

12

14

the other, and this has become even less noticeable in the course of time. As raw edges of the geometric shapes had been turned in during the process of making and were prepared already for *hemming,* it was usual to join these shapes into the required pattern before applying them—as for example, in figure 14 and so only the outer edges needed to be hemmed. Swags and bows of ribbon, and flower motifs cut from templates were prepared in the same way and hemmed into position (11, 12); the *hemming* was done with a white thread and neat stitches on the right side, which in no way spoiled the good appearance of the work.

Original motifs other than those inspired by the printed designs were used for applied work and perhaps the most consistently popular was the *heart* pattern. Evidence of it

occurs in mid-eighteenth century work (p. 35) and from then onwards it appears in all manner of patterns, applied or geometric, up to present day, especially in marriage quilts and coverlets (pp. 35, 59, 61), in those made as gifts (known as *friendship, presentation* or *album* quilts in America) or in work made by, or intended for, children. Because of the difficulty of presenting the pattern in geometric patchwork, it is found generally in applied motifs, two eighteenth-century examples of which are illustrated (15, 16), and also patterns from children's and adult work of the nineteenth century. Later in the century, household objects, farm and domestic animals and birds, silhouette figures and numerous other patterns which occurred to each individual worker were introduced.

15

16

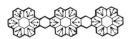

17

Other methods used in applied work were those in which the stitching was done over the raw edges of the patterns, which were cut always from printed designs. *Herring-bone* stitch seems to have been the most popular (17), with *blanket* or *buttonhole* stitch as second choice (18), and in both cases the raw, cut edges were tacked down first and the stitching worked over them; both stitches were worked on the right side. Sometimes the tackings have remained in the work, whether with intent or forgetfulness is not certain, but with either process the effect is more decorative and the results as long-lasting as those achieved with hemming. Herring-bone stitching nearly always was done with a white thread so that the outline was merged into the background material; buttonholing, on the other hand, being a closer stitch inclined to emphasise the outline of the motif, especially when worked with a coloured silk thread, which was common.

The use of embroidery stitches has been limited and when present, generally was confined to applied work. In eighteenth- and early nineteenth-century work, the addition of simple *stem* or *outline* stitches was intended to emphasise fine detail only, such as a tendril, a small spine (p. 39) or a fine, curving stem beyond the capacity of the average needlewoman to accomplish in applied work. About the middle of the nineteenth century, embroidery in silk and metal thread was used in *Crazy work* to such an extent that the patchwork was almost obliterated; *ribbon* work also was applied lavishly, especially in borders of quilts made of silk and velvet pieces (p. 71). In recent years, very simple embroidery stitches in traditional applied work have been popular once more in the eighteenth-century manner; the stitches used are intended to emphasise detail, or obtain an effect such as the eye and the crest of the Lapwing (p. 93).

The most popular arrangement of patterns in early quilts was that in which an elaborate design, usually enclosed in a border pattern, took up the centre of the work and often was of large enough proportions to cover the bed from the foot to the pillow; this was sur-

18

rounded in turn by one or more borders of varying widths, until an outer one completed the work. Second in favour was the all-over design, in which only one border pattern enclosed the main pattern at the edges. The Levens Hall quilt is an example of this (p. 33) and also a coverlet composed of *hexagon* and diamond patches enclosed in a border of applied floral motifs, made towards the end of the eighteenth century (p. 41). It will be seen, though, that even here the centre of the work is emphasised by a slightly elaborated arrangement of hexagons; but this has been a common practice in all-over patterns of all periods, possibly so that it should act as a marker for the middle of the patchwork when more than one person was concerned in the making (pp. 89, 91).

The formula of a centre pattern enclosed in a series of borders was common to English and American quilts and was open to so many variations that its popularity is not surprising. In England there is no traditional description of the type, but an American quilt made in this way, illustrated in Mrs. Ruth Finley's *Old Patchwork Quilts and the Women who Made Them*, is described as a 'framed medallion' pattern and in recent years and from this the name, 'framed quilt' seems to have been adopted in England. This type of pattern is found in all kinds of patchwork; it may consist of geometric patterns only (pp. 35, 43, 45, 54), of applied work only (pp. 51, 57), or of a combination of both (p. 37), and its persistent popularity created a fashion and a demand for the commercial production of specially printed patterns, for use as centre panels in applied and patchwork coverlets. An earlier English fashion for printed panel designs—often octagonal in shape—dating from about 1798, for use on upholstered seats

and backs of chairs, may have been the inspiration for this demand, but so far none of these eighteenth-century panels has been identified in patchwork.

The quilt panels seem always to have been floral in character and several of them in surviving quilts were those printed to commemorate national events, and so, presumably, were used almost at the time in which they were printed. Two illustrated examples are believed to have been used in the years which they commemorate; the earlier bears the inscription 'G 50 R', beneath a basket of flowers and the national emblems of England, Scotland and Ireland (p. 43) and commemorated the golden jubilee of George III in 1810; the second print was made in commemoration of the Duke of Wellington's victory at the battle of Vittoria in 1813 (p. 45). Another and even more popular panel was printed in 1816, with roses and Prince of Wales' feathers among the designs, and is inscribed PRINCESS CHARLOTTE OF WALES TO LEOPOLD PRINCE OF SAXE COBURG MAY 2 1816. Each panel was enclosed within its own printed border and it was possible to buy cottons printed in stripes of matching border patterns of greater width, which could be sewn on without further trouble; a matching outer border of the *acorn and oak leaf* pattern in the George III quilt can be seen.

Other decorative designs, not primarily intended for patchwork, nevertheless were exceedingly popular. From about 1815 a number of printed cottons showed game birds under different kinds of trees, of which several have survived in patchwork quilts. Peacocks and pheasants are shown in two bedspreads illustrated (pp. 47, 48); another pattern of partridges under a flowering plum tree has survived in another two quilts at least, but

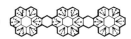

undoubtedly the most popular was that of a cock pheasant standing beneath a palm tree. In two coverlets (pp. 47, 48) made about 1820 this motif has been used lavishly in partnership with the peacocks; in one design the 'pheasant and palm' is seen as the centre motif and in the other coverlet, which was made as a pair to the first, the motif is used five times in a flower-strewn ground; every leaf and flower is in applied work and each motif is hemmed separately to the ground. The same 'pheasant and palm' pattern appears also in an American quilt illustrated in Mrs. Finley's *Old Patchwork Quilts,* another instance of the close connection between English and American patchwork at the time.

During the period from 1795 onwards, the use of dark-coloured cottons is a characteristic of the patchwork. For the last five years of the eighteenth century, dark backgrounds were fashionable for dress and furnishing prints and their influence can be seen in the clear definition of the geometric patterns, especially in English work.

About the middle of the 1820s, the character of the patterns and their arrangements began to change. The fashion for coverlets and applied work gave place to quilts and bedspreads of heavier make composed of geometric patchwork. At first the most popular shapes continued to be those in which the patches could be made by systematic folding and cutting of square or rectangular pieces of material, such as the *square, triangle* or *pyramid,* the *diamond* and even octagonal and hexagonal shapes. There is little evidence of templates having been used for shaping the pieces much before the middle of the nineteenth century, but the later craze for complicated patterns brought the need for greater accuracy and from about 1845 onwards,

templates were looked upon as work-box equipment. Presumably some mathematical plan must have been used for the patterns in the coverlet on page 54, made between 1838 and 1842, although it is conceivable that paper-folding or compass drawings were the basis for them, with the paper then cut into small numbered sections and covered with fine silk pieces.

Until the change in character, coverlets had been used as day-covers for the beds in well-to-do houses (p. 35), concealing the warm quilted covers beneath, for which patchwork was used in poorer or thrifty households without any day-cover. The process of quilting on patchwork is difficult to do because of the uneven thickness, and much of the beauty of quilting is lost on any but a smooth surface. In the mining communities in the North of England, quilts were made of a number of squares or *blocks,* half of them composed of patchwork and half of plain calico (pp. 20, 21); the most elaborate quilting subsequently was done on the plain squares, but the expert workers were not deterred by the patchwork, and many patterns have fine work within the patchwork (pp. 58, 61). Strips of plain material were used also, alternating with strips of geometrical patchwork the full length of the quilt, to make a pattern of broad stripes; or, as in the quilt illustrated on page 57, the strips sometimes were arranged around a centre panel, with quilting on the strips and following the patchwork. A Durham *marriage* quilt contains applied and patchwork patterns, with quilting following the patchwork and on the wide border (p. 58), but where the worker had not been expert enough to work on a quilting frame, a quilting stitch often was run round the outline of the patches to

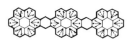

hold the top and lining together (p. 81).

A number of patterns on block quilts of the nineteenth century are common to English and American work, notably the *basket* which has lent itself to so many variations (2). Two English types are illustrated in figures 5 and 6, and two American—the *Garden Basket* (p. 77) made of coloured calicoes, and an embroidered silk and velvet version, in a quilt of 1845 (p. 53). The similarity of the patterns and the different treatment of the same subject make interesting comparison. Some other patterns in work of both countries are adapted from quilting motifs of the same name—*Star, Heart, Feather,* and variations of the *Rose,* dating from the nineteenth century.

The block method of constructing a bedspread is simple and has the virtue of covering the ground effectively with a comparatively small amount of work, but this type of quilt-making has almost died out in England because the art of traditional quilting has nearly vanished also; but in the United States and in Australia fortunately this is not so, and there are more present-day quilts in those countries which merit their name, than do the so-called quilts in England, which more truly are bedspreads or coverlets.

Since the early years of the mid-nineteenth century, the English preoccupation with the hexagon shape has been such that the 'honeycomb quilt' has become the most typical of the country's work. The patterns have a precision and charm not found in those made from other shapes, when they have been thoughtfully planned, but delightful and promising patterns have had a way of petering out into a sea of confused colours without this care. A bedspread made with hexagon patches of a size which usually is

popular—about 1 inch to 1 ½ inches across—needs upwards of 3,000 to 4,000 pieces, which is quite a formidable undertaking even with the determination to see it through, but without it or without the help of several workers it may never be done. In the leisured days of the last century much time could be given to the plan of a bedspread before the work began, but nowadays it seems that the apparent difficulties of planning a design, controlling the colours and pattern and the seemingly endless work ahead, defeat many good intentions. There are however simple methods of making a good design, which not only are traditional but also economical in materials, time and work, if the need for a plan or lay-out is accepted as the first stage. Traditional ways of doing patchwork should be studied and as many as possible are illustrated from which present-day materials, methods and ideas can be adapted.

GOOD MATERIALS will ensure the longest possible life for a bedspread, but it is a mistaken idea that the best way to do patchwork is to buy a number of lengths of new material expressly for the purpose of cutting them into small pieces and joining them together again. It is not possible always to gather together sufficient pieces to make a bed-cover from dressmaking or furnishing left-overs, as patchwork calls for a selected variety of materials of good quality and in good condition; there is a subtle difference of character in the work for which a certain amount of contriving has been needed, and in that consisting of materials specially bought and in unlimited supply.

Women's magazines, especially in America, offer materials and patterns packaged ready for making a quilt, but it seems that

this defeats the chief purpose of patchwork, which is to make use of unwanted pieces, and is liable to produce a sameness in the work and deprive each quilt of the individual character which is half the charm of patchwork. An insufficient supply of coloured pieces usually is the worst problem, but it always has been, as can be seen by the ways and ‘means used in the earliest patterns. It can be seen also, that plain calico was the means by which the coloured patterns were dispersed in a suitably contrasting background, whether they were made of patchwork or applied work.

Bleached or unbleached calico has an unbroken tradition of use, not only as a background material for applied-work coverlets and geometric motifs but as a lining for all bedspreads; most of it was unbleached when the work was done, although much is white now through time and use. Unbleached calico nowadays is cheap to buy and can be had in a variety of widths up to 112 inches and in light- and heavy-weight quality. For the service that is required of it, it is the least expensive of any cotton fabric; that it is hard wearing can be proved many times over by the numbers of quilts and coverlets surviving over the years, which often are held together by the calico linings and foundations but its highest recommendation is that it lends itself to every process of applied work or patchwork, and is most accommodating and pleasant to sew. Bleached calico is equally good, and often preferred, and some workers like to wash unbleached calico before using it.

Tradition has shown also, that pure cotton or linen are the best for all patterns and among those which have been proved are calico, chintz, piqué, sateen, casement, twill, marcella, damask and poplin, whether in dress or furnishing weight. During the last ten years or so, some French and Swiss furnishing cottons have been used; Swiss percale in particular has good natural colours in the flower and bird patterns.

It cannot be said too often that all materials should be chosen for their good quality; inferior stuffs are not worth considering as they will produce only inferior results. Quality in texture should be combined with good fast colours, as the periodic washing of most bedspreads is a normal occurrence and colours which run are useless and can ruin the work.

The nineteenth-century combination of silk and velvet proved to be uneconomic, partly because it was impossible to wash and partly because the two fabrics were not sufficiently alike in weight and texture, and the quilts did not wear well. Silk of superfine quality would be satisfactory on its own, and so would velvet, but the time taken to collect enough of the right quality might be longer than that needed to make the bedspread; smaller things such as cushion covers and the like, made of good silk, would be preferable to a bedspread in silk of uneven quality.

Although rayon is hard wearing when used in the piece, it has proved unsympathetic to patchwork processes and to applied work. Synthetic materials, at present, are of no value as too many are semi-transparent and all are very difficult to control, fraying badly when cut and unsympathetic to handle when making the shapes.

THE GENERAL PLAN for a bedspread can be drawn up before or after the materials have been collected. Which comes first depends on the individual, but it is wise to do both before the actual work is put in hand.

The size of the bedspread, whether for a

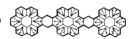

single or double bed, is the first thing to decide and there is no better way to plan and arrange the whole work than to do it on the bed for which it is intended, where this is possible. A white sheet spread over the bed and pillow makes a good 'drawing-board' for planning the position of the centre pattern, if there is to be one, or if not, for marking the centre of the work; for deciding the depth of the outside border pattern in relation to the height of the bed and whether the spread is to hang to floor level or not, as well as for any other points to note in the lay-out of the patterns.

Whatever pattern is decided, it is as well to quarter the 'drawing-board' by folding it into four and marking the position of the folds by tacking with a coloured thread; other marking lines can be added if necessary as it better to have too many than too few, especially when planning for applied work, as nothing can spoil its good appearance more than for some part of a design to be out of place, however slight this may be. The background material itself can be used as the 'drawing-board' for the planning when it is being made of applied work.

As the work progress, each motif or section, when it is tacked into shape and ready for joining, can be tried out in position first. The view of a quilt in a flat illustration is not that which will be seen when it is on the bed and a trial placing of each part of the design as it grows, in a horizontal position, gives an opportunity for second thoughts and adjustments.

Many bedspreads in the past have been made with border patterns on three sides only, on the assumption that the pillow end will be out of sight when it is turned over the pillow (pp. 87, 95). Undoubtedly this is an

economy if some pieces are in short supply, but it does mean that the pattern is not reversible and there are obvious disadvantages in a bedspread which cannot be changed from end to end occasionally.

Some designs lend themselves to a square shape and these are particularly suitable for a double-bed size; rectangular spreads are better for a single bed, especially those with a headboard only. A traditional plan for a square coverlet which can be adapted to almost any type of work is illustrated in figure 19; the patterns can be arranged

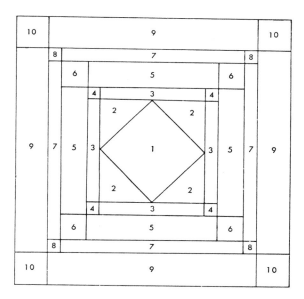

19

1 Centre panel of printed chintz or applied work on calico
2 Corners of printed cotton or applied motifs on calico
3 and 7 Strips of plain or printed coloured cotton
5 and 9 Geometric patchwork or applied patterns on calico
4, 6, 8, 10 Squares of plain colour or white with applied motifs

around a centre as suggested in the key to figure 19, and alternated with borders or strips of uncut material. A round or oval shape can be substituted for the square centre and the strip borders at the sides can be lengthened, to accommodate a coverlet of rectangular shape. This kind of plan for a coverlet was that for which the commercially-printed panels were made (p. 43) and it is one of the best methods of covering a comparatively large area with the least amount of sewing. True, the cotton printing factories in England to-day have not (as yet) risen to the occasion and produced the decorative panels and borders which were so much in demand 150 years ago; nevertheless, there is an abundance of all that could be desired in printed furnishing and dress cottons to make to-day's bedspreads equal to any in the tradition. There seems to be an unlimited choice of large motifs on furnishing prints suitable for the centre piece, and very little imagination is needed to find suitably patterned cotton prints which can be used for the strip borders.

Different methods of constructing quilts are with block patterns, in which each square is completed before joining, and the *Log Cabin* and *Crazy* types in both of which the pieces are joined to build up the fabric, but both the latter require an applied work technique as the pieces are overlaid on one another and sewn on the right side, whereas geometric pieces are inlaid and joined on the wrong side. *Log Cabin* patterns depend on the arrangement of light and dark colours without a plain background, of which an American *Barn Raising* quilt illustrates one of the many examples of this kind of patchwork made during the nineteenth century (p. 79). *Crazy* patchwork sometimes was sewn to a

backing material the size of the bedspread, but more commonly the pieces were sewn to square sections of strong backing and joined later, as in the Welsh quilt illustrated on page 71.

Log Cabin and *Crazy* patterns are rarely made nowadays. They are somewhat cumbersome to handle and the finished quilts are heavy when made with the traditional fabrics for the types—silk and velvet. Cottons have been used from time to time for both, but the results have been poor and no compensation for the labour involved.

The block quilts on the other hand lend themselves to almost every type of geometric and applied work. The size of each block or square in a quilt is identical in size—traditionally they are from 12 to 15 inches square —each containing its own complete motif, and there are few identical quilts to be found, even in the *basket* pattern (pp. 53, 61, 63, 67, 69, 73, 75, 77). The squares can be arranged in a straightforward chequered

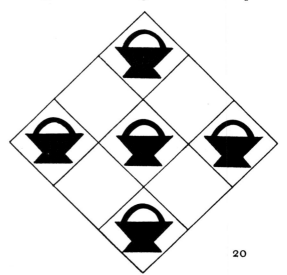

20

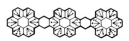

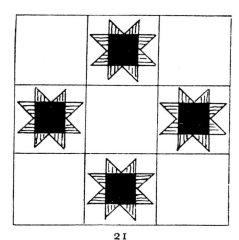

21

pattern set straight with the edges of the quilt or diamond-wise, often to suit the shape of the motif (20, 21); in some designs a strip of figured material is inserted between the blocks (p. 63). Traditionally the alternate squares are quilted only, but for the unskilled in quilting, each square may contain a motif and the lining attached to the top by tying or knotting, or by a running stitch round each motif (p. 81). This reasonably quick and simple block method of quiltmaking is rarely followed in England, whereas it is universally popular in America.

THE USE OF COLOUR in needlework of any kind has its problems and in patchwork, where the choice is confined to the colours of the materials available, forethought and planning is equally as important as the arrangement of the general design, so that the proportion of colour and background is well balanced. Most of the traditional designs consist of the repetition of one or more motifs and if the area of the work has been quartered, so can the amount of coloured pieces be divided into four and the proportion to

be allowed for each quarter be estimated.

As in previous centuries, fashion influences to-day's patchwork with the stronger and brighter colours which are being worn and used in furnishing. Cottons in general are of good quality in texture and colour, and a number of furnishing materials contain printed designs on dark grounds resembling those used in quilts of the early 1800s. Dark colour has the virtue of intensifying the quality of both bright and pale colours in the quilt patterns; examples made as far apart in time as c. 1825 (p. 51) and 1964 (p. 95) are evidence of this. A rabble of coloured pieces in geometric patchwork can be brought to order if enclosed within a clearly-defined outline of colour (pp. 41, 89, 91), but the principle of enclosing a variety of patterns in a network of one colour can be adapted to suit nearly all types of patchwork (p. 63).

Black has shown signs of coming back into favour. It has not been popular since the last half of the nineteenth century, when black velvet and black silk taffeta were used in complex geometric patterns with a mass of rich bright colours, as well as delicate blues, pinks, yellows and mauve (p. 54); within the last few years designs in black and white, black with grey and white, or black with scarlet and white, show signs of increasing. An American block quilt of the last century, made in black and white only, is an example of simplicity and elegance which would be hard to fault (p. 75).

Block quilts made in the North of England and in South Wales generally were made of one colour and white, especially the interchange patterns made on the principle of the Windmill illustrated on page 65, but the *basket* and other traditional patterns were

made with the same simple colour combination. The all-over *Windmill* quilt illustrated is an example in rose-red and white calico (p. 65); usually solid colour of one shade is used, but variety and a greater economy results if two or more shades of one colour are included—such as light to dark blues, pink to red and dark crimson and so on—regardless of whether the materials are printed or plain. If some relief is needed in monochrome colouring, the addition of one other colour in contrast is made.

Other traditional patterns are carried out in two colours only, especially the striped quilts, in which a stripe of patchwork in shades of purple, lilac and lavender prints, alternates with plain material of a buff-yellow, or bright and delicate pink patches with a stripe of light blue, but there are many others to suit individual ideas and available materials. Not every bedroom calls for a bedspread with a light coloured or white background and another alternative which has been successful for an all-over pattern is that of a small white or light coloured repetitive motif, set in a dark ground.

BORDER PATTERNS are included in nearly every design, whatever the method of work,

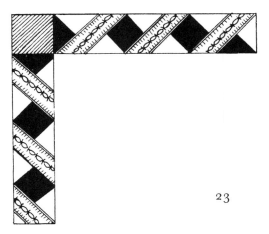

23

and although Log Cabin, Crazy, Striped and some block quilts sometimes have no border pattern (p. 79), there seems to be no hard-and-fast tradition about this (p. 73). All other types of patchwork and applied work patterns are enclosed in border patterns and without them most bedspreads would seem incomplete.

The border should be considered from the beginning as part of the design, not added as a makeshift use for the pieces that are left over, but if the centre pattern and the border have one distinctive thing in common, such as repeats of a motif or a definite combination of colour, the design is united. The *Star of Bethlehem* quilt contains a link in centre and border patterns, in the identical construction of both and is an excellent example of planning (p. 37). Other illustrations contain methods of planning a border as a continuation of the pattern and at the same time as a termination or 'boundary fence' to the work. Some early nineteenth-century patterns were bordered with wide uncut lengths of cotton print, not always to the improvement of the design (p. 43); others were finished

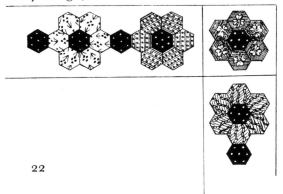

22

24

with lengths of calico decorated with applied motifs (p. 41).

Turning the corners of any border pattern may be a difficult matter without careful measurement and calculation, and a common solution for many patterns has been the insertion of a square piece the same width as the border, into each of the four corners. The square may be made from a coloured print, or if there is a border of geometrical motifs, an isolated unit sometimes is applied to a plain square; in a border of linked *rosette* motifs for instance, a single *rosette* is applied (22). Two other examples of turning a corner are illustrated (23, 24).

A geometric border pattern known as *Dog's Tooth* which was popular for applied work coverlets, is illustrated on pages 39 and 51; although the pattern has the appearance of being made from triangular pieces, often it was made from a strip of material attached to the edges of the foundation, and then cut and folded into shape; this was a simpler method than using geometric patches to get the same effect. Strips of the required width and long enough to extend along each side of the coverlet were needed and if, say, the points were to be 4 inches deep, the strip was 4 ½ inches wide to allow for turnings. It was then tacked along the coverlet edges, with the right side of the strip to the wrong side or back of the coverlet, and joined by a run-

ning stitch about ¼ inch from the raw edges (25 a). This join could be done by machine nowadays.

The unattached edge of the strip was then marked at 8-inch intervals (c), and at each mark the strip was cut at right angles to the edge, to a depth of 4 inches, to b. Next, the strip was turned on to the right side of the work and the cut edges folded neatly back (c to b) using d as the pivot. The folded edges were then tacked into position and hemmed down (b to d) leaving the lower points about ¼ inch from the outer edge of the coverlet (25 b).

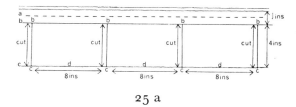

25 a

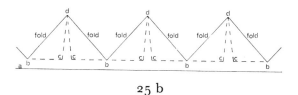

25 b

Accurate measurements are needed to achieve a neat corner with this border, but the square patch again is a satisfactory alternative (p. 23). Patterns which present difficulties at the corners sometimes are worked from a planned corner towards the middle of each side and the resulting hiatus, if any, is filled with the date of making and the name or initials of the worker (p.24).

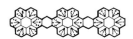

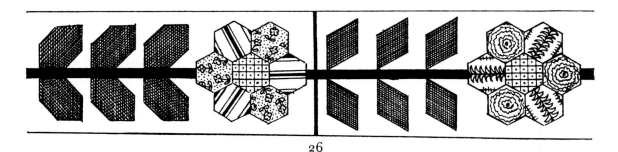

26

Applied work borders can be as elaborate (12, pp. 47, 48) or as simple (pp. 61, 73, 95) as the pattern demands. The use of natural outlines, such as leaves or formal leaf and flower patterns in geometrical shapes (26 to 28), is a traditional and often appropriate way of decorating a border. Both can be a means of using a number of colours to good effect, as each repeat of the same motif can be different in colour or of two or more colours combined. The *leaves* and *stems* of floral patterns can repeat the main dark colour in the design; or the colour can be introduced into the border as illustrated on page 95, where the arcading is made from the same dark chintz as the tree and leaves in the centre pattern.

LININGS should be attached to all bedspreads in geometric patchwork, so that the raw edges on the back of the work are covered; coverlets decorated entirely with applied work usually remain unlined, as the foundation is the lining or backing for the pieces. Light-weight cottons make good linings, even for silk patchwork, and calico, scrim and sateen have withstood years of wear and tear in early work, so this should be their recommendation. A used sheet, an old cotton counterpane or other similar material, also has been used from time to time.

All the papers having been removed from the patches, top and lining should be tacked firmly from end to end, and side to side, while they are lying flat on a table or on the floor, unless the work is to be quilted. If quilting is not possible, an interlining such as a thin blanket, flannel or domette can be substituted for the carded wool or wadding used in quilting, and this must be inserted and tacked into position with top and lining. There are two methods, both simple and

27

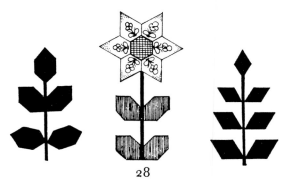

28

effective, of joining the top and lining other than by quilting; one is by *knotting* or *tying* the two, or three, layers together at regular intervals; the other is by making a *running* stitch around the patches or sections of the pattern (p. 81), both of which add decoration to the design when done carefully.

JOINING THE EDGES of the top and lining is the next process; it is an important part of the work and should be included as a part of the general design. It should strengthen the work also at the edges where the first signs of wear usually appear. Although there are several ways of finishing the edges, those which have been proved to be the best are the following:

a) Running together the turned-in edges which is a traditional process used for quilt edges.

b) Inserting a covered piping cord between top and lining, and hemming on both sides, which is a stronger and neater method than running one side and hemming the other; this is the usual method.

c) Binding the two edges together with ma-terial of a matching or complementary colour in the design.

d) With a fringe (pp. 35, 53). A fringed edge hardly ever is used nowadays, in spite of it being suitable for almost any type of bed-spread and not only for coverlets, and as a finish it deserves more consideration in the plan of work.

SIGNING AND DATING present-day work of any kind is an important part which is omitted all too often, and modesty on this score should be overcome for the benefit of posterity, no matter how elementary the work may be considered to be, and even to the anonymity of initials and year being hidden on the back. The correct places are either on the centre panel or on a border pattern and a proper inscription should include the day, month and year of finishing, and the full name of the worker. American *Friendship* quilts are signed on each block by the maker and so each is properly recorded. A patchwork bedspread should be a record of contemporary textiles and as such is incom-plete without the year of making, at least.

THE PLATES

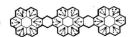

The Levens Hall Furnishings

The bed furnishings of patchwork at Levens Hall in Westmorland are unique in the history of English patchwork. Although the work does not bear any date or signature, the patterns were made from pieces of the Indian prints, imported into the country at the end of the seventeenth century. The workers are presumed to have been the second wife of Colonel Sir James Grahme (who owned the house at that time) with her step-daughters and other members of the household, and it has been a belief of long standing in the family that the work was done about 1708. From the evidence of the materials and the work, and according to good authority, this suggested date 'is perfectly feasible'. It can be seen that the printed motifs are characteristic of Indian work, and the colours, in shades of red and blue and in spite of their age, are remarkably clear. The octagonal and cruciform patches contain quite large uncut motifs from the prints and several are repeated, so that the furnishings present an interesting record of the textiles; the fabric has been well preserved with few signs of the wear and tear which probably has destroyed other examples of patchwork of the same period.

The complete set of the quilt and hangings is made in the same all-over pattern of geometric pieces; a portion of the hangings is illustrated but with the exception of the quilting, the pattern is that of the quilt itself. The greatest economy was used to avoid the waste of any scraps of the scarce and valuable prints, and several shapes are made up from small pieces joined together with much skill.

The quilting on the quilt is stitched in a simple diamond pattern, but a characteristic of it is the red thread with which it was done. Traditional quilting on patchwork is worked usually with a white thread.

c. 1708

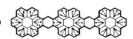

Eighteenth-century Marriage Coverlet

This coverlet is one of the rare examples of an eighteenth-century day-cover for a bed, for which the under quilt, made to go with it, is still in existence and kept with the coverlet.

In some ways, the quilt, which is not illustrated, is equally interesting; both sides of it were made from large rectangular pieces of Indian printed calicoes of floral patterns on a white ground, which were joined by seaming, and with an interlining, were quilted together to make a night quilt, slightly smaller than the day-cover.

The patchwork pattern on the coverlet was designed by a young man from the island of Jersey named Le Patourel, whose occupation was privateering, in a ship which took him sometimes to India. He was a man of many parts and among his interests were cabinet making and a Devonshire girl—a Miss Shepherd—who was a fine needle-woman. The results of their combined interests were that Mr. Le Patourel designed a set of chairs, presumably for the bedroom of their future home, and so that Miss Shepherd was not idle, he designed their marriage coverlet on the same lines as the inlaid woodwork of the chairs. The two were betrothed in 1760, when, so the story goes, the designing was done and the work begun. No one really knows the sequence of events for the next 25 years, but the facts are that they remained faithful to one another for that time, each engaged on their respective work and to one another, and eventually in 1785 they were married and lived happily ever after.

The coverlet is a remarkable piece of work. Dark, richly-coloured cottons are used with patterned white and light colours; the realistic 'woodwork' panels are composed of pieces of sandalwood pink and pale yellow cottons. Probably the method of making the patterns was by cutting out a full-scale drawing on paper, a method often used then and later. Each piece of the pattern was numbered on the drawing and when cut out it was covered with material and joined to its neighbouring numbers. The work is unlined and the faultless sewing can be seen. Not the least elegant part of the work is the 3-inch cotton fringe with which the edges are finished.

Size: 99 ins × 96 ins   1760-1785

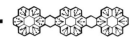

Star of Bethlehem Quilt

The star pattern made from a mosaic of diamond shapes is common to American and English patchwork from the last part of the eighteenth century. Occasionally the pattern in English work is built from hexagon shaped pieces, to make 6-pointed stars.

In this quilt the materials are early chintzes, English calicoes and copper-plate prints, and the colours are arranged to give the greatest effect to the carefully cut pieces and the whole pattern. The *lozenge* border pattern carries out the character of the centre star, especially in the well-planned method of turning the corners, and frames both it and the applied floral patterns. The simple directness of the whole design conceals the amount of skilled work in the quilt.

The work is quilted in a number of designs which fit into the patchwork; diamond quilting is worked over the centre square, leaf patterns are fitted into the triangular spaces in the lozenge border and a *running feather* pattern decorates the white border. The quilt is very old and in a fragile condition, but is held together by the quilting.

Other names which have been given to similar quilts with this pattern include the *Rising Sun* and the *Lone Star of Texas*.

Size: 106 ins × 110 ins   Late eighteenth century

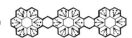

Broderie Perse Spread

The tree pattern on this coverlet could have been inspired by the type of printed patterns of the Indian *palampores,* in which trees with spreading branches contained figures of small animals, birds, flowers, fruit and leaves, and occupied almost the width and length of the beds on which they lay. The cut-out birds and pomegranate fruits on the branches here are similar to those on the *palampores* and in the catalogue description of the coverlet, which is in the collection of the Shelburne Museum in Vermont, some chintzes used in the work are said to have been 'probably cut from an oriental *palampore*'.

Most of the applied patterns in traditional patchwork were cut from partly worn fabrics and stitched to a new foundation in order to preserve them and to provide an inexpensive decoration. An account of the method used for this work is given also in the museum catalogue—'Using a frame which held the foundation material firm so that the stitching of the motifs to a new backing would not pucker, the needleworker made a new spread for herself. The technique was known as Broderie Perse... In America, this style of work remained in vogue until the middle of the nineteenth century. It was so highly regarded in the South that chintzes were purchased just so that they could be cut apart to furnish appliqué designs'.

In order, no doubt, to augment the materials needed to carry out design in this work, the tree trunk and branches were cut from linen and the roots and leafy branches from a home-dyed cotton, which was used also for the border at the edge of the coverlet and for the leaf tufts on the *pineapples*. The flower motifs, cut from printed cottons, have small spines embroidered in peacock green thread added to the stems; the whole work is applied to a foundation of homespun linen.

Size: 106 ins × 107 ins   Eighteenth century

Eighteenth-century Cotton Coverlet

The pattern on this coverlet is an early example of an all-over hexagonal design. The coloured *rosettes* consist of seven hexagon patches surrounded by a row of white, and each is contained within hexagonal compartments outlined by a single row of dark-coloured diamond and triangular pieces. Plain and printed dress cottons were used to make the *rosettes* and this type of arrangement—including a slightly more elaborate centre as a 'marker'—with innumerable variations, has had a constant tradition in England to the present day. During the early 1930s, the same pattern was used in a coverlet made for the Duchess of York (now Queen Elizabeth, the Queen Mother), and several others, including at least one cot cover, are known to have been made.

The contemporary designs on pages 89 and 91 were based on the same idea, but hexagon pieces were used to make the outlines of the compartments and no applied patterns were included. A quilt design of about the same time—the American *Star of Bethlehem*—contained patchwork and applied-work motifs (p. 37) and in the nineteenth-century simple applied patterns, such as the swag or hammock, were used to finish geometric block and other types of patterns.

The applied motifs in the illustration here consist of cut-outs from printed cottons, of sprays of flowers and leaves, and stems of grapes and vine leaves decorate the corners of the borders; in continuation of the work, the applied border is edged with single rows of diamond patches.

There is no name or date on the coverlet, but when it was given to the Victoria and Albert Museum in 1925, it was understood to have been made between the years 1780 and 1790 by the great-grandmother of the donor. Although it is very large, it was not of unusual size for its period.

Size: 120 ins × 120 ins   c. 1780-1790

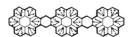

George III Commemorative Quilt

Especially manufactured commemorative textile prints, dating from the end of the eighteenth century, are found in patchwork. The earliest known so far was a blue print on a white cotton ground made to commemorate Nelson's victory at the Battle of the Nile in 1797, in which the name NELSON was incorporated in a pattern of acorns and oak leaves.

The centre panel of the illustrated quilt contains a basket of mixed flowers, beneath which are the national emblems of the Rose, Thistle and Shamrock, and on the surrounding border of acorns and oak leaves on a rich yellow ground is an inscription 'G 50 R', which signifies the Golden Jubilee of George III, who came to the throne in 1760. Although this print does not bear a date the inscription makes it certain that it was manufactured in 1810 and the quilt probably was made in the same year. A wider border, between the patchwork *cotton reel* and double *box* patterns, repeats the acorn and oak leaf design and is an example of the twin prints produced especially for patchwork during that period.

The quilt is in perfect condition and until it was given to the Victoria and Albert Museum in 1961, had remained with the descendants of the maker since it was made; it was wrapped in a linen sheet and probably had never been in regular use. The colours are still rich and bright; many are of the fashionable dark blues, browns, greens, reds and black of the time and provide the sharp contrasts in the patterns which are so much to their advantage. The outer border consists of lengths of a floral cotton print.

The quilt is lined with white cotton and interlined with sheep's wool.

Size: 99 ins × 84 ins   c. 1810

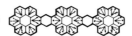

Wellington Commemorative Quilt

Two commemorative panels were printed commercially for use in patchwork quilts, in connection with battles won by the Duke of Wellington. One appeared in 1815 after Waterloo and the other, two years earlier, commemorated his victory at the battle of Vittoria in 1813. The panel is octagonal in shape as compared with the oval George III panel and the narrow printed border surrounding the floral design is of acorns and oak leaves also, but arranged in a series of disjointed motifs. The drawing and colours of the floral design are of the highest quality and the print is in perfect condition after more than 150 years.

The name of WELLINGTON stands out in black letters on a background of the flames of battle and glory' and on the shadowy ground below in small letters is the word 'Vittoria'.

The design is that of a framed quilt and all the frames or borders surrounding the centre contain patterns made from square or rectangular pieces; even the triangular patches surrounding the panel, as well as those of white calico which form the background to the colour patterns, were made from diagonally cut squares. With the exception of one or two pieces of furnishing cotton, all the coloured materials are dress prints, many of them in the dark colours which are so much in character with the patchwork of the early nineteenth century.

It is probable that this work was done soon after the printing of the commemorative panel in 1813. Although it contains no date or signature, the quilt has remained in the family since it was made and through the last three generations the belief has been handed down that it was made by 'Aunt Lucy Gane', the great-great-aunt of the present owners, who was noted for her 'beautiful needlework' and who lived during the period at which the quilt was made.

The work is lined with cotton and interlined with wool.

Size: 90 ins × 87 ins   c. 1813

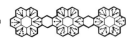

Applied Work Coverlet

The slight variations of pattern in this coverlet and the fellow to it on page 48 were due no doubt to the need for some contriving, in spite of the supplies of material having been nicely judged on the whole. In such detailed work, it is surprising that two coverlets so closely similar were achieved at all. It is clear that although six 'Pheasant and Palm' patterns were available, it was a difficult matter to make two balanced designs and so the resulting division was made, and peacocks and peahens were used to give weight to the coverlet with the single pheasant. A larger number of small bird patterns were included in this design also, 29 of them as compared with 5 in the paired coverlet, in which small flower sprays and vases of flowers were used in larger numbers.

The size of the centre panels vary very slightly; the narrow strip borders are made from different prints and the applied patterns in the second border of each coverlet are rather different in detail, but all these differences are less noticeable when the coverlets are together and the colours of both can be seen to balance well.

The outer borders of flowered prints being alike increases the twin-like appearance of the two, as does the binding of a ribbon braid, with which both are bound at the edges. The size of each is exactly the same.

Size: 105 ins × 95 ins   c. 1815-1820

Applied Work Coverlet

Quilts or coverlets made in pairs are not common and although the two coverlets illustrated here and on page 47 are identical, they were almost certainly intended to be a pair. Both are in perfect condition and neither has had any regular use; on rare occasions they may have been put on the bed for show, and so the original colours have remained bright and both coverlets are complete, as they were made, in every detail.

They were the work of a Miss Caroline Danby, the great-great-aunt of the present owner, who lived in one of the houses overlooking Parker's Piece in Cambridge. The coverlets were made 'in anticipation of marriage' and were put into her bottom drawer for the occasion, which for some reason sadly did not materialise and for over a hundred years now they have been looked upon and admired and returned again to another drawer but not alas, Miss Danby's.

All the patterns were cut from new and unused printed cottons, but they must have been in good supply, as each motif is paired with a nice sense of balance and the possibility of using six of the 'Pheasant and Palm' patterns for the two coverlets does not indicate a very tight economy in materials. The colours which predominate throughout both coverlets are rich reds, blues and greens, although most of the flowers are in the natural colours—yellow and red tulips, pink roses and so on.

It is unusual to see the 'Pheasant and Palm' on a patchwork coverlet with the colours in their original state, as the green generally has changed to blue owing to the fact that the process used to obtain the green was that of over-printing yellow on blue. The yellow, being a fugitive colour did not last, but having been kept from the light since they were made, these coverlets have retained their patterns in their original colours.

All the motifs are cut out and hemmed to the white cotton ground by the process shown in figure 13 and the identical outside borders were made from strips of a floral cotton print.

Size: 105 ins × 95 ins   c. 1815-1820

Applied Work Coverlet

It may not be within the capacity of every worker to design a coverlet of applied work as seen in this example from the early nineteenth century, but to-day's cotton prints, equal to those from which these motifs were cut, are to be had for the choosing of those who wish to do this kind of pattern. The sprays and baskets of flowers are made up from some cut-out with the help of template shapes and some from the printed patterns (4, 11), using bright and dark colours to offset one another and to give a clear outline to every motif. Those around the borders were planned for the hanging position in which they would be seen on the bed, even to the placing of the sprays on the corners.

The patterns are hemmed to a foundation of thick white cotton but alternative methods of stitching could be *herring-boning* or *blanket stitching* (17, 18) which were used for similar kinds of motifs.

The border pattern at the edges of the coverlet, and the medallion of twisted ribbon around the centre flower basket, were cut from a black cotton printed with a red polka dot and the effectiveness of this type of *dog's tooth* pattern for the edges of this coverlet (and the American Broderie Perse spread (p. 39) is clear. The effect of slight miscalculation in the measurement can be seen also in one corner.

The coverlet is not signed or dated, but it is said to have been made about 1825.

Size: 110 ins × 110 ins   c. 1825

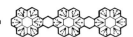

Flower Basket Quilt

As an elaborate version of the *flower* or *garden basket* pattern, this quilt is composed of 13 square blocks containing *basket* motifs, and 12 triangular pieces of embroidered flower patterns. The foundation material is white silk and the work is done with coloured silks and raised or padded applied work.

The blocks are joined to 3-inch bands of embroidered silk, with a *strawberry vine* design, while the outer border of the quilt consists of a 7-inch band decorated with a *running vine* pattern.

The quilting with which the top is joined to a foundation of coarse muslin is remarkable; it is worked in very fine *running* stitch following short straight and curved lines, which give a close crêpe-like effect to the background of the patterns. It is said that 1,001 skeins of silk were used to do the quilting.

The work is lined with rose-coloured silk and the edges finished with a knotted silk fringe.

This is a beautiful example of work done by a young girl, as it was made in Baltimore, Maryland, in the United States of America by a Mrs. Mary Green Moran, when she was a bride of only 18 years.

Size: 120 ins × 120 ins   1845

Nineteenth-century Silk Coverlet

The silk coverlet illustrated is a part only of the original work. It was made between the years of 1837 and 1844 near Yarm, in the North Riding of Yorkshire, in the years during which her children were born, by Ann Hutton-Wilson and her husband Robert. Mrs. Hutton-Wilson was said 'to have no eye for colour and so her husband arranged the bits for the quilt'. He was an artist by profession, which probably accounts for the precision of the planning, but the translation of the design into patchwork, in which the pieces were inlaid and joined on the wrong side by seaming, could have been done only with phenomenal skill and patience. It is doubtful if it could have been made in anything but the fine silks which it contains. The 16-point star in the centre was made from pieces of the embroidered wedding dress of Mrs. Hutton-Wilson's best friend.

The Hutton-Wilsons had three children, Phillis, Robert and Eleanor, and about 1870 the coverlet was divided by removing the yard-wide border and re-making it into a second bedspread; this was taken by Eleanor for her double bed at the time of her marriage, and which she used until it was worn out in the early years of the twentieth century. Phillis kept the centre of the coverlet, which was handed down later to a daughter of Robert Hutton-Wilson, the present owner.

There is no indication as to the method used to make the pieces with so much accuracy but they could have been drawn with geometrical instruments. Early patterns of this type, such as that of the coverlet on page 35, were made by drawing a full-scale design on stiff paper, numbering each section down to the last detail and cutting it out. Each piece was then covered with material and joined together in the order of the numbered papers, which were left uncovered on the back of each piece. Some patterns were made by paper-folding rather than drawing and the same procedure of numbering and so on was followed. One eighteenth-century floral design done in this way was made over thick grey paper and the numbered papers still remain in the motifs.

Size: 120 ins × 120 ins   1837-1844

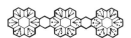

Durham Applied Work Quilt

The applied *flower basket* patterns on this quilt were made in Weardale, Country Durham, by Mrs. Isabella Cruddas in the middle of the nineteenth century and are unusal for their period and for their locality. The baskets are unlike any others found in work of the time or later (5, 6), and resemble more those used in earlier designs; they are not unlike the basket shapes of the Broderie Perse spread on page 39. The flower sprays and some of the flower heads are reminiscent also of work done 50 years earlier. There seems to be a strong relationship between this design and those which were more common in America, although the frames or borders of wide bands of colour alternating with white are typically North Country English.

The general plan could not be improved upon for this kind of applied work. The simplicity of the pattern arrangement is equalled by the simple colouring of red and green dress prints and white calico. The patterns are not crowded and the restraint in the number, proportion and spacing of the motifs is an object lesson. The determination of the worker, to avoid having to mitre any of her corners, is remarkable and consistent throughout.

The economy of work in the applied patterns also was brought to a fine art; except for the centre basket of flowers and those on the four small corner panels, which carry out the same idea, there are only two other motifs—the stars and trilobe patterns which fill in the corners of the centre. All the applied work is done by hemming.

The quilting patterns are even more skilfully worked; they are more elaborate in technique and follow the patchwork patterns, with a *diamond* pattern on all the panels—the centre having an additional border of *roses*—and each of the strip borders is quilted in *worm* or *chain* patterns alternatively.

c. 1850

Rural Industries Bureau

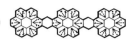

Rebecca's Quilt

Rebecca's quilt was made by Mrs. Rebecca Temperly of Allendale, County Durham, probably for her wedding, and it is said that she wished it to be inherited by the first granddaughter who was named after her.

The general design is unusual, but without doubt it was planned so that the coloured patterns should lie on the top of the bed, and that the hanging sides of the quilt should show the quilting to the best advantage without any patchwork to conceal it. The continuity of the design in both kinds of work is seen in the repetition of the quatrefoil *heart* motifs.

The patterns are characteristic of those associated with marriage quilts. The four single *heart* motifs in the square centre panel are repeated in the quatrefoil arrangements—also supposed to represent the four-leaved 'lucky' clover—in the four corner squares and repeated again in the wide quilted border.

The applied patterns in the centre include a 16-point *star, clover* leaves, curved leafy sprays bearing what appears to be a fruit pattern and small formal *bird* motifs, similar to those seen on samplers of the period, are supported on sprays in the corners. The corner sprays are seen again on the smaller squares, and also the *clovers,* quatrefoil *hearts,* and small 8-point *stars*.

The quilting is finely worked in short, close stitches, following the applied motifs in the centre panel and in *shell* pattern on the small squares, with fan motifs in each corner. The deep white border consists of quilting only; a *twist* pattern borders the patchwork centre and the diamond-set squares on the following border enclose the quatrefoil *hearts,* with leaf patterns in the triangular spaces.

The patchwork and applied work is done in coloured dress prints and the ground is of white cotton.

Size: 108 ins × 108 ins

1860

The Christmas Bride Quilt

Heart motifs in quilting and patchwork are included traditionally in work that was made to mark the occasion of a marriage or an engagement, the birth of a baby, or as a gift for a child, especially for girls.

The shape lends itself to applied work more than geometric patchwork, although it has been included in marriage coverlets made in this way from time to time. In two English examples made by prospective brides and illustrated (pp. 35, 58), the hearts are made in solid shapes, as compared with the outline motif used in this quilt in the collection of the American Museum in Britain, at Bath.

In America, marriage quilts have had more social significance than at any time in the English tradition. Girls were supposed to have a number of quilts—a dozen was a comfortable dowry—which were made during their early years, and the marriage quilt was not begun until a marriage had been arranged. When the initial construction was done, the final quilting was worked at the now well-known *quilting bees,* parties at which the friends of the engaged girl gathered to put the finishing touches to the quilt, often enough adding hearts to their quilting patterns.

This quilt has been given the name of the *Christmas Bride* as 'the holly motif suggests a Xmas wedding'. It is in fact of a size more suitable for a single bed and as a rule, marriage quilts are larger and more elaborate than the everyday double size. Could it possibly have been a Christmas present for a child? Be that as it may, nothing is known of the maker or for whom it was made, except that it is an unusual design and shows imagination and delicacy in appearance and colouring. The *hearts* and *holly leaves* are of a faded green cotton, with bright scarlet *berries* scattered liberally over the motifs. The swag border also is in red and green and the outer edges are bound with red cotton.

The quilting patterns are of *stars* within the *heart* motifs, *feathered crowns* in the intervening spaces and *running feather* on the swag border.

Size: 75 ins × 72 ins   Nineteenth century

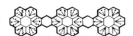

Chintz Diagonals Quilt

American *friendship* quilts are composed usually of a number of block patterns, each made and given to a member of a community by his or her friends to mark a special occasion. This has not been a common custom in England, although in the North of the Country a son or daughter often received the gift of a quilt from the mother on the occasion of his or her marriage, but there was a 'veritable craze' for friendship quilts about 1850 in America, which are known also as *presentation* or *album* quilts. Some quilts contain the signature of the makers on each block.

The arrangement of the bouquets and garlands of flowers in this quilt, in the collection of the Shelburne Museum, is an example of careful work, well thought-out, although the blocks were made by different workers, several being signed and dated. In the Museum catalogue the designs are described as being 'stitched around the center or along the outlines of the blossoms, and on some of the flowers running stitches separate the petals or veins of the leaves, thus giving a puffed appearance to the motifs'. Some of the applied motifs have been attached with close blanket-stitching, emphasising the outlines, and the work is finished with a handwoven braid binding at the edges.

The diagonal lines of print intersecting the blocks and half-enclosing the small sprays of flowers in the triangular spaces just inside the heavily flowered border, gives continuity to the design made up of so many different motifs. The quilt is in perfect condition and when it was acquired by the Museum a card was sewn to the back bearing the inscription—'Specimen of home-laid-work and very fine quilting. Done in Pendleton, South Carolina'.

Size: 102 ins × 113 ins   Mid-nineteenth century

Windmill Quilt

The Windmill pattern seen here was made in Weardale, County Durham, and is typical of a number of traditional patchwork quilts made in the North of England and in South Wales, which consist of what are known as interchange patterns. The patches are not always triangular, although the *windmill* and the *cotton-reel*, some versions of the *tree of life* or *tree everlasting* and the red and white *basket* are made from them; the *jockey-cap* and *pincushion* contain circular motifs which require more skill than other shapes. *Robbing-Peter-to-Pay-Paul* is an alternative name for several of these patterns in England and America.

Two-colour patterns often are made from printed dress cottons such as pink and blue, lavender and blue, purple and a yellowish buff, as well as each of these colours with white, but they are rarely of plain colours, except Turkey red. The rose-patterned red cotton used in this *windmill* quilt has mellowed with wear and washing and is now a deep rose colour; the white calico patches are still fresh and white, a characteristic of this material, which seems to improve rather than deteriorate with washing.

This quilt, like others of its kind, is one which is seen at its best on a bed. The border is particularly effective when it is in a hanging position and the traditional quilting patterns with which the patch-work is quilted enrich the design when it can be viewed in a hori-zontal position.

The lining is of white calico and the interlining of wool. The edges were finished by turning in the sides of the top and lining and running them together; this is a traditional method of working the edges of quilted bedcovers.

Size: 87 ins × 77 ins   c. 1890

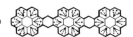

The Princess Feather

The *feather* pattern is one which undoubtedly originated as a quilting pattern. It is common and popular in English and American work, whether in applied work or quilting, and in each case there are many variations, the *feather crown* or *wreath,* the *running feather* and the *feather,* arranged as the spokes in a wheel and illustrated here. It has been suggested that *Princess Feather,* which is an American name and not used in England, may have been inspired by the feathered headdress of an Indian princess. Used in this arrangement, sometimes the ends of the feathers are incurved, so that each resembles a question mark, but the American feather in applied work as a rule is a more exuberant and lively affair than the English version.

The *Princess Feather* is a large pattern always, and this version seems to need more room on the quilt than usual; the quilt is composed of four blocks only, each measuring 29 by 29 ½ inches instead of the customary 12 to 15 inches, and the 7-inch wide border decorated with *feathers* in pairs, seems quiet and modest compared with the block patterns. *Feathers* in applied work usually are made in two alternate colours; this quilt is in red and green home-dyed cotton on a white ground and other popular combinations are red and yellow, or green and yellow—often in printed cottons—and always on a white ground.

The quilting patterns are worked in the spaces between the feather motifs with *pineapples* with a feathered outline and the remainder of the ground is filled with an all-over *shell* pattern.

The quilt is known to have been made before the middle of the nineteenth century and probably is a comparatively early example of the pattern, as most of the surviving *feather* quilts seem to have been made towards the end of the 1800s.

Size: 78 ins × 78 ½ ins   Before 1850

The Meadow Lily Quilt

The *Meadow Lily* pattern contains three sprays of a flower motif which is made of one triangular patch and four diamonds, which appears to have more different names and associations than any other of its kind. According to the American State in which it was made, so it was given a different name—*North Carolina Lily*, the *Mountain Lily* in Kentucky, the *Mariposa Lily* in California, and in Pennsylvania and Connecticut, the *Meadow Lily*. There are several other names, for what is virtually the same pattern, in other States. When the three sprays are attached to a *flower pot* pattern, it is called the *Lily* or *Flower Pot* and other very similar flowers in the same arrangement are called tulip patterns. The five patches which make the flower, without the stems and leaves, sometimes are arranged to make patterns with names as dissimilar as they can be from lilies and tulips but are self-descriptive, such as *Bear's Paw* and *Duck's-Foot-in-the-Mud;* in Philadelphia it is the *Hand-of-Friendship*.

In this quilt the sprays of lilies are made from pieces of red or green cotton prints, instead of the home-dyed plain red and green cotton, and all the patterns are applied to a white ground with hemming. The blocks are slightly smaller than is common in a quilt of this size, being 11 inches square, and a *bow and swag* border is joined to the quilt round the blocks.

The quilting is done round the outlines of the patterns, as there is no space between the lilies for a separate quilting pattern.

Size: 90 ins × 88 ins   Nineteenth century

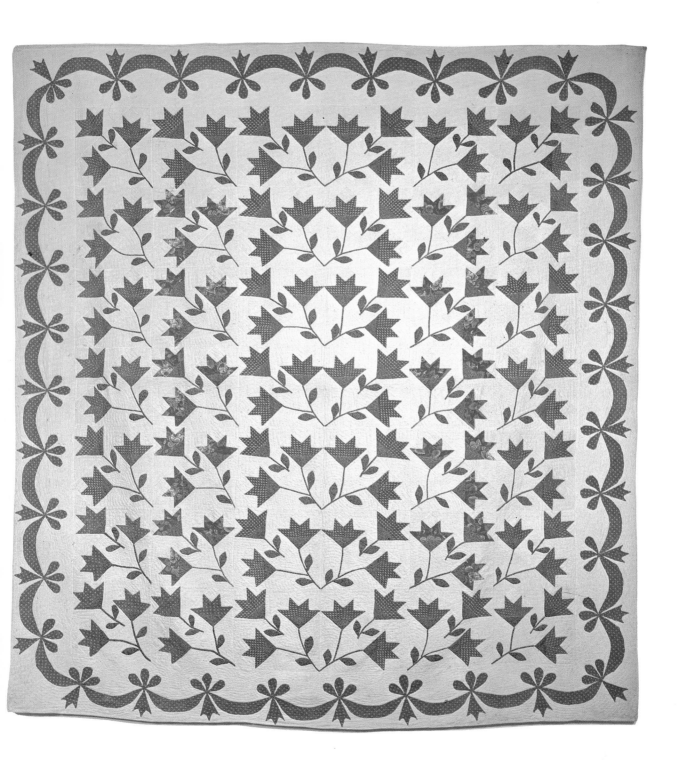

Crazy Quilt

The so-called Crazy patchwork, which had a period of great popularity during the last 30 years or so of the last century, had the distinction of reaching on occasions the heights of near perfection in planning, colour and needlework, as well as the lowest depths of each. The theory of joining pieces of any shape, colour or kind to make a quilt, is more simple than the practice of so-doing and there is only too much evidence to show how often the practice has failed; but when a good example of this work has been preserved, the reason for its appeal can be understood. The quilt illustrated was made by a Welshwoman, Miss Jenny Jones, towards the end of the nineteenth century and is one of those which reached the heights. It won the first prize in a quilt competition in Chicago in 1884, when Miss Jones was living there, and has everything that is needed in Crazy work.

In the first place, it was made of good quality stuffs, so avoiding the common mistake of thinking that 'anything will do for patchwork'; also, the pieces were well proportioned in size and the colours well distributed. The figured brocades and velvets were dispersed evenly with the plain pieces, and the embroidered flower and bird patterns worked with skill. Many of the flowers are done with ribbon work, and strands of silk, attached by one end to the body of a Bird of Paradise, were meant to represent the flowing elegance of the tail plumage. One mole-coloured scrap of velvet, figured with small curled feathers, has attached to it a slip of paper with the words written on it—'Father's Wedding Vest'.

The patchwork was made in nine square blocks and joined together. The border surrounding them is itself a feature of the work; the material is a dark green mossy velvet, which was decorated with a waving pattern of rose buds and forget-me-nots in ribbon work.

Size: 72 ins × 70 ins   1884

Wreaths and Flowers Quilt

A block quilt of 16 sections in which no pattern is repeated exactly, is a typical example of the many quilts made in this way, in a tradition which is wholly American. Any similar patterns on quilts in England so far, have been found to have an American origin. In the illustrated quilt, the simple taste of the worker can be seen in the variations of the patterns and in the arrangement of an individual piece of work, although it represents also a type of American friendship or album quilt, which is quite different from the one shown on page 63, the *Chintz Diagonals* quilt, in which a number of workers took part.

The patterns here were cut from plain coloured cottons in the primary colours as compared with the floral print cut-outs in the other designs. Each formal flower, fruit, leaf and stem shape is cut individually and arranged to compose a wreath or bouquet, and then hemmed to the foundation of each block.

The name given to the design is descriptive of the patterns, and some of the wreaths consist of fruit patterns of grapes and cherries —always popular in applied patterns—as well as simple flower shapes. In some blocks the flowers are shown in arrangements with vases, and four others show sprays and bunches of flowers and leaves.

Some of the motifs were attached with blanket stitch, the method shown in figure 18, and the fine stems used to attach the cherries and grapes to the bunches were worked in chain stitch with blue thread, in the same method used in the *Garden Basket* quilt on page 77. The quilting is worked in the spaces between the patterns, in a *feather wreath* design and the quilt is finished at the edges with a red cotton binding.

Size: 90 ins × 90 ins   Third quarter of the nineteenth century

The Widow's Quilt

The chief characteristic of this block quilt from New Jersey in the United States of America, lies in the economic severity and elegance which are combined in the sharp outlines of the black motifs on the very white ground and the broad mourning band of black which borders the design.

The reasons given for the name of the design is that the black motifs signify the black darts of death, and the single bed size of the quilt denotes the bereaved state of the sleeper. The quilting pattern stitched on the alternating white blocks carries the thought embodied in the title a stage further, as each is of a memorial *harp* or *lyre,* as elegant in outline as the *dart* motifs.

The *dart* motif appears to be of eighteenth-century origin in American patchwork, although the name given to it in this quilt is a comparatively recent one. Mrs. Ruth Finley refers to the earlier pattern as the *Palm Leaf* and the *Hosanna;* she heard of it first in the State of Main, and later found a 'very faded, stained and tattered remnant' of an early quilt, in which the *palm leaves* were arranged alternately in facing and reversed pairs, without the intervening white blocks as in the Widow's Quilt.

In the illustrated quilt, the blocks are unusually small, measuring only 7 ½ inches square, each set diamond-wise in parallel rows. The pattern is equally effective in a reversed position.

Size: 93 ins × 86 ins   Nineteenth century

74

The Garden Basket

An unusually rich buttercup yellow cotton was used with white to make the *baskets* in this American version of the pattern, instead of the more conventional red and white of the tradition when it is made in geometrical patchwork.

This type of *basket* to which flowers and fruit have been added is an understandably popular one as a means of combining geometric patchwork with applied work. Not only can it involve the use of highly technical needlework for those with the necessary skill, but it can be made with the simplest processes of sewing and still produce a good pattern. For all its simplicity, this example of the *Garden Basket* was made with considerable skill in fine sewing.

Although the fruit and flower patterns can hardly be said to fill the baskets, their position, poised over the top of each, almost wills the onlooker to believe the baskets to be filled to overflowing. The predominant colours are green (all the leaves), two shades of yellow, and red, with some small additions of a faded pink in the cherries and one basket of apples, where the motifs have been made by joining pieces of the two shades to give an effect, presumably, of a 'rosy cheek'. The grapes are in a lighter shade of green than the leaves and are joined to the stem with embroidery in chain stitch; the same method of working the fine stems is used for the cherry stalks and so on and the stouter stems are applied strips of green cotton. Some of the fruit is *raised* or padded to give it more substance.

Most of the quilting is worked in *cross-diamond* pattern, except underneath and on both sides of each basket where the spaces are filled with *bars* and surrounding the fruit and flower motifs a fine *ripple* pattern is worked, which is used in the silk *basket* quilt on page 53.

Size: 75 ins × 88 ins   Nineteenth century

Log Cabin — 'Barn Raising'

Log Cabin quilts were popular in England and America from about the middle of the nineteenth century, and were so called because the square blocks were composed of a square centre patch surrounded by strips of material or 'logs', which were overlapped at the corners in much the same fashion as the log cabins were built. All kinds of material were used; many early examples were from strips of woollen fabrics, as well as cotton, silk and velvet. Towards the end of the century in England, they were made from odds and ends of silk and velvet ribbons when these were highly fashionable decorations for dresses and hats; the quilts were known as 'ribbon quilts'.

It will be seen from the diagram (19) and illustrated quilt that the patterns are dependent on a repetitive arrangement of colour in the squares, which are always divided into light and dark shades. The overlapping layers appear to give a third dimension to the patchwork, as well as a sculptured effect to the pattern because of the illusion created by the colour arrangement.

Quilting in patterns was almost impossible through the several thicknesses of the patchwork, but the lining was attached only to the back of the work as a rule, either by a quilting or a tying stitch which did not show at the front.

Although each square is made on the same principle, the arrangements vary to give a different design; all are known as Log Cabin quilts but the several variations have different names, such as the 'Barn Raising' illustrated or 'Straight Furrow', in which the colours run in diagonal stripes across the quilt. In England, the name Log Cabin has been the name given to all arrangements, although the work is done rarely nowadays.

Size: 80 ins × 80 ins   Last quarter nineteenth century

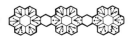

Honeycomb Coverlet for a Doll's Bed

This honeycomb coverlet was made for a nineteenth-century doll's bed and illustrates a piece of work in small scale, showing all the manœuvres necessary in making a similar coverlet for a full-sized bed.

As far as possible the printed patterns were in proportion to the size of the patches and the white background materials were chosen for the equally suitable texture, also having in mind the size of the patches. Piqué of exceptionally fine ribbing, a small patterned dimity and fine linen, taken from stiff shirt collars and fronts, were chosen; the latter was, of course, boiled before cutting out in order to remove all the stiffening.

The colour prints were cut from an unused nineteenth-century Cobden print with a patterned ground, bearing rose and cherry motifs in red, with small brownish leaves and black stems. Red spotted cotton pieces were used to relieve the white background occasionally and the outer border consists of a single row of the rose print, alternating with patches of dark red cotton. The patchwork is applied by hemming to a surround of white linen, which is finished and joined to the lining with a red covered piping cord. In order, as far as possible, to keep a regular serrated edge to the pattern, pentagon patches were used alternately with hexagons on the side borders.

The work is flat quilted—without an interlining—with a double row of *running* stitch round each section of colour and following the outer row of patches; this gives the effect of raising them slightly from the background and makes a good finish. The coverlet is lined with a patterned print matching the ground of the coloured rose and cherry motifs in the patchwork; matching linings were a characteristic of the work done at the Cobden factory.

Size: 15 ½ ins × 13 ½ ins   1936

Northern Night Quilt

Canadian patchwork is unfamiliar in England but quilt-making has had a tradition there since the time of the first settlers and most patterns originally had a British or American origin. In recent years there has been a noticeable development of individual design, understandably somewhat American in style.

The Northern Night design breaks new ground and is a striking example of simplicity and economy in present-day design and colouring. The use of a repetitive pattern of a single native species of bird makes interesting comparison with other contemporary bird designs on pages 93 and 95, and the feeling of the immense space and loneliness of the bird's habitat in conveyed by the background. The reversed natural positions of the Pole Star and the Great Bear can be overlooked quite happily on the grounds of poetic licence. An embroidered panel on the back of the quilt records that the designer was Miss A. B. Torrance, and the makers 26 members of the Simcoe Arts and Crafts Society, and that it won a prize of 500 dollars in a cross-Canada quilt-making competition in 1956. Later it was bought and presented to the Royal Ontario Museum.

All the materials are cotton, of which there are seven shades of plain colour and one black and white print. The Loon and stars were made from the print which was used in uncut strips for the outer border; each bird has a black bead for an eye. The rest of the pattern is made of coloured cottons ranging from lemon yellow to a deep yellowish green, which represent the Aurora Borealis, the sky and water; these are seamed together and the star and Loon motifs are applied. The Pole Star consists of a black star motif applied over one of yellow.

Quilting patterns are worked in relation to the areas of patchwork. Straight lines follow the direction of the Aurora, on which star patterns are scattered also, and a *wave* or *ripple* pattern is worked on the *water*. The quilt and lining are bound at the edges with white cotton.

Size: 96 ins × 74 ins   1956

Honeycomb Coverlet

This example of a honeycomb coverlet is one of a pair which were begun after the Second World War, during the period when the rationing of clothing and materials was in Britain still controlled by the allocation of personal coupon allowances to individuals, and this prohibited the use of any new materials in the patchwork. The work of making the coverlets was undertaken by members of Womens' Institutes in the counties of Dorset and Somerset, as a contribution to the furnishing of a room at the adult education college sponsored by the headquarters of the organisation.

The materials for the coverlets were collected with difficulty and it was not possible to supplement the contributions of used cottons with bought materials, even for the linings.

The flowered and coloured prints were in scarce supply for making two coverlets, but to compensate for this, interest was added to the pattern with the use of several kinds of white cotton—piqué, damask, marcella, linen, calico and so on—and by the arrangement of pieces of different textures a subsidiary pattern was built up of white materials, which occupied the areas of background between the coloured patterns. A spot pattern of single hexagons of a 'rosebud' print was used to break the otherwise all-white background.

The centre panel was bordered with a waving band of floral cottons, planned to surround the top outline of the bed, and the remaining coloured pieces were joined to make as deep an outer border as the materials would allow. The coverlets were lined with damask table-cloths and finished at the edges with covered piping cord. The diagonally shaped corners were planned to prevent damage to the coverlets by falling on the floor at the foot of the twin beds, as the space between them was limited.

The linings were attached to the patchwork tops by *knotting*. The work on the illustrated coverlet was done by 58 women from 11 villages in Somerset.

Size: 108 ins × 78 ins   1948-1950

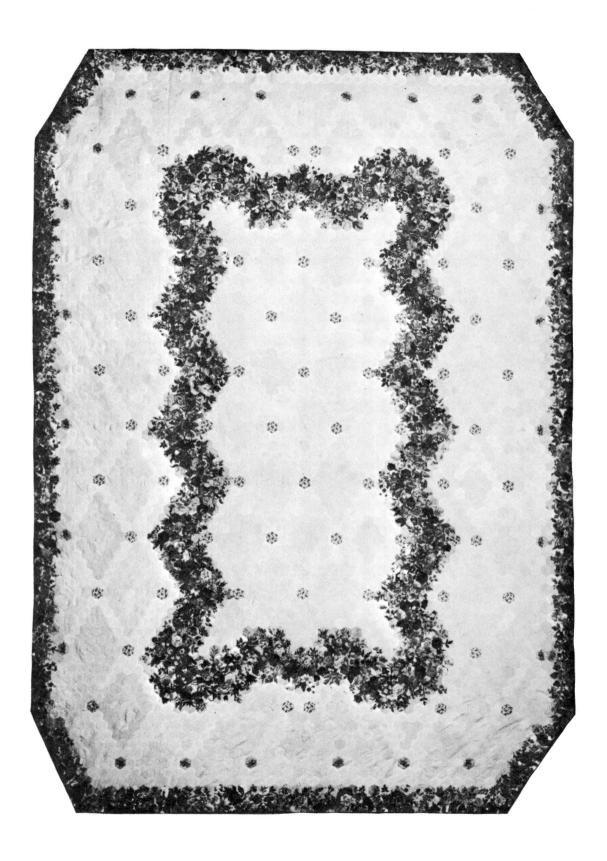

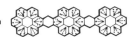

Miniature Bed and Coverlet

The honeycomb coverlet illustrated was made for the miniature mahogany bed on which it is seen and both are part of the furnishings in one of the scale model bedrooms in a collection of miniature furniture owned by Mrs. Carlisle at Ashampstead in Berkshire. The carpet, also to scale, on which the bed stands was made for the same room.

The hexagon pieces were cut from early twentieth-century flowered cotton dress prints, and contemporary percales for the blue background colour. The centre panel consists of a coloured border surrounding a rectangular compartment which fits the outline of the top of the bed and a coloured motif decorates the pillow area. The border pattern is one of the several versions of the *Ocean Wave* which has been a popular English border pattern since the last half of the nineteenth century. In this version, wavy lines of different coloured patches, sometimes shading from light to dark colours, ran along the edges from top to bottom and across the ends of the work; other borders were made of short wavy lines running at right angles to the outer edges of the quilt. There are a number of variations, but the characteristic wavy line is seen in each, in whatever direction the lines run.

This coverlet was made in the conventional shape for bedspreads intended for four-post beds and a square space was left at the two corners at the foot of the bed, so that the cover fitted snugly round the posts and hangs evenly at the sides and end of the bed. It is lined with light blue percale and bound at the edges with the same material.

Size: 10 ins × 13 ins   1958

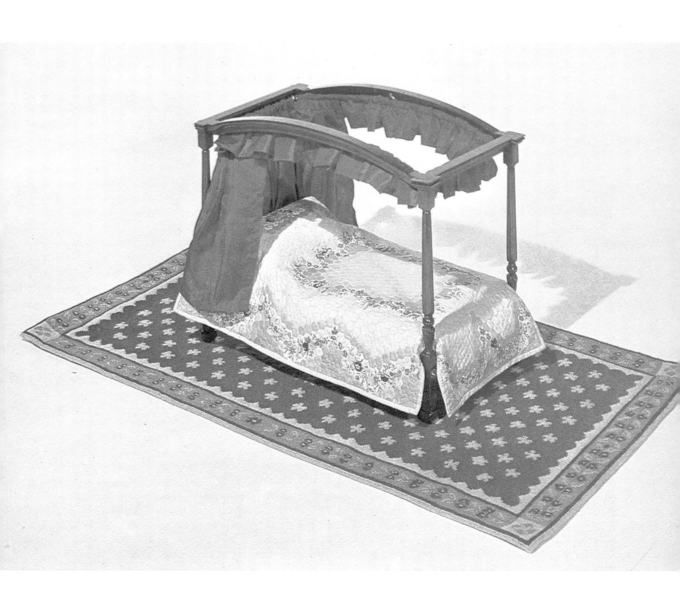

Honeycomb Coverlet

Here illustrated is a honeycomb coverlet in which a variety of coloured motifs are contained within hexagonal compartments, giving the appearance of a block quilt. The hexagon patches used for the outlines of the compartments were cut from a French percale, printed in a striped design of blue ivy-leaves; the outer strip border is made from lengths of the same material, mitred at the corners, and the repetitive use of this print gives the dominant character to the design. The background colour is that of a pale green and white pinstripe cotton print.

A patchwork border pattern, with an uneven outline and roundels at the corners, is composed of a collection of floral prints. It is another example of a border which is seen to the best advantage in a hanging position on the bed; the flat view does not do it justice. The patterns within the compartments were constructed in matching pairs to give a fair balance to the design and the central motif, as usual with this kind of design, is somewhat more elaborate and different from the rest.

This coverlet owes much of its character to the fact that it is made in the true patchwork tradition and most of the materials were collected over a period of time from various sources. All are of furnishing cottons and chintzes in scraps and unused left-over cuttings from the making of chair covers and so on; the bought material was that for the background and the French percale—a justifiable expense in order to carry out a good colour design.

Size: 90 ins × 66 ins   1960

Blue Diamond Honeycomb Coverlet

The design of this coverlet was built on the plan of the eighteenth-century example shown on page 41, but with the use of hexagon patches only, instead of combining them with the diamond and triangular shapes used in the earlier work. The compartments differ also in that they are lozenge-shaped rather than hexagonal, for the reason that the proportions were more suited to those of a cover for a single bed instead of for a double bed, which usually is square or nearly so. An applied work border was not attempted as not enough floral prints suitable for the work were available.

The amount of other materials, however, was adequate enough to allow for a greater amount of coloured pattern in proportion to the background and so the size of the *rosette* contained within each lozenge was increased by 12 patches into what is known traditionally as a *double rosette*. The centre motif, or 'marker', also was heavier in design and different from the others, although the flower print included in it was repeated throughout the whole design.

The design had a controlled colour plan; the scraps were collected by the workers from dress and furnishing cottons among which blues predominated, largely due to the summer fashions of the previous year or two, and so flowered cotton prints and striped, spotted and check ginghams in which blue, red and pink were included were chosen. A certain amount of dark blue poplin was bought to supplement the supplies of that and dark blue linens which had been collected. The white background materials included linen, calico, piqué, damask and casement.

The coverlet was made in the traditional manner by a number of workers, from the Somerset villages of Broadway and Horton, each being responsible for sections made in their homes—the double rosettes, small triangular units, and strips of white and dark blue pieces, were so prepared.

The work is lined with white calico bought for the purpose and the edges are finished with a red covered piping cord. The patchwork is attached to the lining by knotting.

Size: 106 ins × 84 ins   1959

British Birds Coverlet

Bird patterns of exceptional quality have been used on the inset panels of applied work in this patchwork coverlet. Bird motifs in earlier work generally were cut from printed patterns, but here appropriately coloured and patterned prints have been used for each part of the bird. A drawing or tracing of each motif was made and was then cut into sections—such as wings, tail, body and head—from which pieces of Viline were cut out and covered with the appropriate materials, thus using the same kind of technique used in the eighteenth century. Viline is unaffected by washing and can be left in the work.

A drawing and sections of the Lapwing pattern (in the top left hand panel) is illustrated (7, 8) as an example of the section cutting. Each section is reassembled by applying it in position on the foundation, overlapping the one beneath sufficiently to be hemmed to it; wings usually are added last, unless they are in a flying position.

Embroidery is used for fine details; beaks and legs are worked in the appropriate colours, using long and short *filling* stitches; eyes also are filled in according to the size and where necessary; outlines —such as the white body of the Lapwing—are worked in a single line of *stem* stitch. The crest of this bird also is embroidered.

The background of each panel is cream linen, to which the birds are hemmed. Among those represented are the Lapwing or Green Plover, Puffin, Mallard, Robin, Canada Goose, Green Woodpecker, Kestrel and Oyster Catcher; the centre panel contains Golden Eagles.

The patchwork is made from hexagon and diamond pieces in dress prints of dull pink and lilac on a blue-green ground, and others of predominantly dark bluish green. A single line of diamond patches surrounding each panel, and the covered piping cord with which the work is finished, are of dark green percale. The lining is of unbleached cotton and carries the date and signature—'British Birds. D. M. Crampton. 1959'.

Size: 92 ins × 54 ins   1959

Tree and Birds Applied Work Coverlet

A formal type of tree pattern, as a focal point for a collection of naturalistic bird patterns, has been used for the design of this patchwork coverlet made by the worker of the coverlet on page 93. As with the other work, printed cottons were chosen which most closely represented the natural colours of each bird and each motif is shown with insight into the stance, character and behaviour of the bird.

The *tree* is made entirely from dark green percale, three template sizes being used for the *leaves*, for which the basic shapes were cut from thin Viline, covered with the percale and left in the work. The bird patterns were made in the same way; the very slight padding of the Viline gives a little substance to the motifs and eliminates the 'dimple' in the middle of each, sometimes caused in thin materials, when turnings have been used at the edges. Fine detail was added by embroidery for the beaks, legs, and eyes and for the pendant crest of the Heron. Other birds represented are Osprey, Chaffinch, Swift, Jay, Great Grey Shrike, Cuckoo, Roller, Robin, Waxwing, Blackbirds, Kingfisher, Wren Nuthatch, Pheasant, Green Spotted and Lesser Spotted Woodpeckers, Golden Oriel, Bullfinch and Blue Tits.

The base of the *tree* is set in a mound made of *shell* patches. The pieces are approximately 4 inches across and made of multi-coloured prints in green, blue, yellow and brown.

The arcaded border is outlined in strips of dark green percale and the spaces decorated with natural leaf shapes, some are green and others in Autumn colouring; the texture and colours of the materials, as with the birds, were chosen to represent the natural leaves as nearly as possible.

Unbleached calico was used for the foundation, to which the *tree* was attached with *slip* stitch and the bird motifs by *hemming*. The work is signed and dated on the back—'D. M. Crampton. 1964'.

Size: 100 ins × 86 ins   1964